Sunsets Over Cityscapes
Poems for the Existential Uprising

Ty Gardner

Feed a man a line from a poem and revive his soul for a day. Teach him to pick up the pen, and his words will change the world.

Table of Contents

Poems for the Existential Uprising

Scattered moments of wine reflection
and thinking over things I overthink,
      I could've been a giant,
colossal even,
could've placed my hands
      on a hundred million hearts
and healed the whole of existence,
but here I sit,
      writing poems for the existential uprising instead.

Reasoning My Reasoning

By spall and loam and peppered brow,
the crescent form of a half-tide shore speaks on your behalf,
but I'd know your voice even in the crash of breaking swell
beneath the gaze of lighthouse luminescence.

"Come to me by way of park bench dreaming,"
you say, and I oblige.

Would you reason me unruly if I themed a thousand
of these stories around the silk of your porcelain tones,
a thousand more of the wetted earth illuminating the ink-black
of your Snow White strands, or the passion passed down
by your father's mother?

Would that be unreasonable?

Canyon Mouth at Dusk

Canyon mouth at dusk,
the skyline west is a wolf,
      supping the setting sun,
          sluicing slivers of moonshine,
              guttural and godawful.

Shadows settle in the shallow
of river bends a-curve valley roads,
and the night is on us—quaking Aspens scatter in the headlamps
as we drive.

Dust in the Hutch

"The longer you live, the more you lose."

Gran must've said that at least a thousand times over buttered
breakfast toast and half frames,

and I get it now; understand about dust in the hutch and why plastic
Christmas trees in cobwebbed basement corners never come down.

Flower Wilt and Pocket Lint

Flower wilt fragrance and pocket lint,
coppered bits and fingertips,

      nighttime's for nightcaps and processing the oppositional;
for pulling the untethered ends together with Paloma pick-me-ups
and bedding them down.

      Being brave's tomorrow's business,
      not for nighttime.

We Press Our Sins in Tomes

Make no mistake, mistakes were made;

the past never dies for a poet,
we never bury the hatchet,

but wield our pen as a poleaxe and press our
pecanncies into paragraphs,
    compile everything into colossal tomes and bundle them against
their brothers on burdened bookshelves.

Apologies

Apologies to skipping stones,
to muddy banks betrenched by careless boyish boots,
and the refractory consequence of disturbing still waters.

My condolences to killing time with petty pastimes and finding
fulfillment in austerity—I've never felt more alone as I do now.

Love Language

Never one to hold a hand,
      entertain an embrace, or accommodate affection,

    I spoke my love in the language of a lighting storm,
in the tumultuous tones of thunder and rumble.

    See my heart coming from the incalculable, then count the seconds
corresponding before we collide.

A Time and Place for Quiet

What words to say when your raven slate turns to beach white,

and I feel you slipping, course as speckled sediment from coastlines
afar, pebble tick by pebble tock through palms assailed of angry
undercurrents—when the lamplight of waxwork skies burn and fade,
what words?

Today, Be Bold

Brave a branch or two today,
and scale your Sycamore youth.

Behold the terra firma from above, how it's just as you'd imagined,
but not as you recall, and climb.

By virtue of looking back on deserted dreams and reveries of dashed
desires, be bold and brave a branch.

Put It Down in Pantomime

Put it down in pantomime,
the misplaced pain of pressure,
the tire, and tug of toxic personalities,
the polarizing pull of Gibbous moons,
and the peculiarity of pondering the proper pronunciation of

        affect and its effect,

and tell it all to the tune of a Texas rain cloud.

People Are More Interesting as Poems

Never enough for anyone; I'm too in love with everyone.

Smitten swiftly by a speaking voice, the soft lines of kind eyes call
me—like lamp lights that waft and glide in Thai night skies,
I'm captivated and can't be helped.

Invisible in ignorance, illuminated in poetry.

A Nod to the Tree I Misspoke Of

A nod to the tree I misspoke of in the sulk of November mood swing,
confess to my cynical conjecture.

Madmen shoulder the shame of speaking too soon and steady their
grief in pride of pleasing poetry—that tree spills my secrets to the
spring Sparrow now without regard.

People Don't Make Changes

People don't make changes, they make choices; change comes from
consequence in the face of confrontation.

I remember anecdotes of passing notes,

   four square flirting,

and surrendering to Simon's stipulations.
Before the brainwash of constructs spoon-fed to me like cereal.

Every Body Prays the Same

Twenty-three when she came to me
 (a glass bottle bodied beauty),
studious and steadfast in spirituality,

I taught her my religion—movements in midnight mass and tributes
to each other's Temples.

Sensuality our scapegoat;
we kept the faith in folded arms and fawning eyes.

Tell Me Not to Love You

Summon us somewhere we can't refute, late nights 'neath lamplights, double-doors on dilapidated domiciles in the new of old Orleans, toe-to-toe where rainbows go or rain-sacked patios singing things only God knows.

and I won't

Tell me not to love you, ˄   ˄, but leave me the illusion.

Heaven Doesn't Need Another Casualty

God,

   grant me the perfect line, something about the importance of
keeping the faith in the face of my turmoil, standing tall in the saddle
when my haughty high horse endeavors to eject me, anything to keep
me from courting curtains—heaven doesn't need another casualty.

When You Tell Your Mother About Me

Praise and say the name of your Holy Father
when you tell your mother about me;
when you lock your eyes to mine
and speak a love prayer in a language from lands of old.

The words won't be known to me,
but the sentiment will shine through—
as the sun does even in darkness.

Something to Be Said of Selfishness

Twenty-something in a time-lapse throwback, savoring the sunrise at
hyper-speed, sitting with myself, having a word to the wisdom of

selfishness and wild oats sown,
the leisure in being lazy
and letting that bell ring long into the coming decade
until the echo catches us.

The Charm of Childhood Homes in the Country

Rooftop raindrops call for quiet,

call for calm,

and keeping things to yourself; rapped-tin on the charm of my
mother's childhood country home taught me that.

If I had a dollar for every time I knew the burden of rainless rooftops,
I'd buy that house and keep to myself.

Whispered Words Are My Weakness

Whispered words
      are my weakness,
hushed tones against
      the thirsty tug of tusks on
my left earlobe light me up
      and get me flowing like oil
lamps down the Ganges—
something ceremonious in the lack
of vibration
      from the vocal cords.

Religious, the prayer of whispered words.

Sealing Secrets With a Kiss

We're talking tongue-in-cheek these days,
tucking our taste buds into pockets of tissue,
prodding,
pressing our passion against sheets of sinew,
and writing our refrain in the white of lips pinched by craving canines.

Oh,
the things you do to me with your demure demeanor.

September Comes Calling

September salutations
and the shy of summer sizzle,
cooling on the courtesy of a telephone call,
      restless at the hours passed,
running on recycled hope, a wing and a prayer request
      that she'll come to her senses,

recall me cute in September salutations and ring me back.

Strangers in the Silence

Some say the shadow knows,
      can sense itself being drawn into the spirit world
in the dusking days
      that precede a person's passing.

Shaman speak of strangers drifting restlessly in the still of the silent
hours, speaking something unknown between souls and shaded things.

*Add This to the Others

A longer list now of perfectly practical things
never understood before:

- where men go when they're wide-eyed and silent

- how I'm too much like my grandfather to lollygag

- the distance between death, giving life, and the value of legacy

- the wisdom of the written word

Some Will Gather to Remember (Part One)

Encircled of their
>son and daughters,
grands, and good spirits,
>best friends will come together to share a laugh,
shake a hand,
>and shed a tear.

The neighbors will take up the cooking and cleaning in show of
communal camaraderie as the end draws near—Godspeed, my friend.

Hope Is Holding On

Between a tethered tug on tightrope tension, balancing acts,
and braving an abyss,

between slow hands and quicking sands,
the golden glow of wheat field sunsets, and the tuck back of jet black,
between the shatter of a jaded heart's soft

    "so long"

is me holding on to hope.

Rain and Run

Rain and run.

Round down to the nearest thousandth of a million memories
spattered casually as condensation across the causeway of a life cycle
and absolve yourself chaste in the sustenance of a single dewdrop.
Raise a rosary redemption to the scatter of

rain, and run.

Compliance

Spending time tonight in the emptying end of a wine glass
　　　where the wallowed things are,

swimming and swirling a constellation
　　　in guilted half glasses of reneged reparations,

processions of my prejudice whirl-pooling and waiting, slowly
soliciting me to swallow;

　　　I comply.

Contemplating My Memoirs Early

Contemplating my memoirs early,
in case I'm killed comically—ironically, but anticlimactically.

"Life's a tragedy, son, live by the pen, die by the pen; wield your
words as a weapon and spill the ink of your enemies,"

my father'd offered in generous, drunken affection.

Time and Circumstance Taught Me Clemency

These leaves,
such dutiful sons and daughters of mothers' remiss,
how promptly they offer their stalks skyward,
unaware they've long been dormant,
deserted to the indelicate whims
of bodily spoil.

I'd known them eponymously
          once,
as only children can
before ambivalence.

Noble Pursuits Are Pointless

Bitter bit to swallow,
conceding the contrast in breaking the cycle and becoming the cycle;
lo, I do concede such things.

I concede now to the significance of my existentialism
on the insignificance of the infinitesimal,
and the notion that noble pursuits are pointless.

Fantasía: The Dreamer Wakes

Forgive me as I walk my fingers around the outline of your upper lip;
you blush,
      throw me a pair of eyes,
paradise,
        seduce me slow, en Español, "y yo desesperado."

"Perhaps you said so in a dream?"

"Quizás, amore, could likely be."

The night is young, spirited, I awake.

I'm of the Wind

Confessions of a
father,
brother,
husband,
son.

Peculiar how I'm all these things and none.

I call the wind Mariah, and she lulls my choleric constitution.
How curious, the quickness at which I'd abandon everything I hold
dear. Adoration is a habit, and I'm of the wind.

Some Will Gather to Remember (Part Two)

Silent strides on a.m. beaches,

        California's never going to be the same.

Plumeria porches weep in the midnight moonlight,
and somewhere in the still of sullen L.A. sands,
daughters of their mother's mothers ponder banana pancakes as
ocean waves describe evening's events.

We Were Broken Long Before the Jelly Jar

April brisk has summoned me to a standoff. Accosted my constitution with the effrontery of scowling brows, crinkle-creased as crumpled paper, a practiced tradition imparted of my mother's disappointment at my inclination to settle and by her mother before her—long sigh.

Long sigh in the silence as the glass drops, and I brace for impact. A moment of anticipation hangs loosely, and I recall the raucous slap of Smuckers against the kitchen linoleum of a basement apartment I'd long forgotten. Glass and jelly stain settle in my youthful scramble to sanitize—I shudder.

Shudder as I settle in the shallow of memories wallowed—the crush of sandcastle cave-ins at the insistence of guffawing currents and how it felt to know that disappointment for the very first time. Shudder as I backstroke in the still of pooled frustration and regard the ripple effect of dashed dreams.

Sexual Syntax

A touch of down throttle when you tell it to me again,
the part about our pronouns pressing against the verb

    like three little single-syllable sentiments strung together in
sentences of structured sincerity,
                     and run it back a thousand times over as
balcony banter music.

The Young Ones Lived As Giants

Wild abandon won out when I was a wee bit more reckless—
when time, and tide
      collided against disregarded desert dirt drives at dawn.
How we whooped into the Mojave morning nothing,
     a vacuous
space, soundproof as the solar system itself,
I gave my spirit to the stars then.

One

One
for the beat of a drum and every bad girl I bent over
backward to break my best intentions for.

One
for Cupid's eros
and parading my passion precipitously,
for the feel of a fold of a dollar bill between my fingertips.

One
for the one before,
        this one,
the next one.

She Was a Cashier, Young, and I Wonder

Quaint,
the way we quietly condemn particles and pieces of people
          as tidy piles
into the pitch of cornered psyches.

I think of the girl with the lotus flower
          pressed
into the fold of an exposed shoulder and sigh at the subtlety of
parking lot lips and where she is now.

I Might Ask These Things Aloud

"And what of abandoned things? I might ask aloud, to cricket winds
and the general malaise of summer swell;
of vacant valley towns and their unkempt gardens?
Of stars aimlessly afloat,
bereft of incandescence?
Of photo album optimism and how we're covetous?
I might ask.

I Swallow My Truth by the Light of the Fire

Two thoughts come to mind,

throwing back bottled things in fireside speculation:

how you shouldn't've put me in a place between ulterior motive and ultimatum, and how I shouldn't've pushed your patience.

Truth is, I live for the longing, the lusting, and that's my vanity.

Dead Girls Don't Write Postcards

Promise when you put it down in a postcard
that it won't be personal,
that it won't reflect an ounce of regret or indite a single
anecdote about the curvature of back roads at sunrise.
Reassure you rest in peace
and suppress no hard feelings of resentment when you write.

For Later

For when you're older,
for when you're old enough to know better,
but not too old to take things for granted.

For every time we took sides,
drew lines, pulled up our proverbial ponytails,
and put each other through rough patches,
sparred with spiteful syllables, for then.

I'm in No Rush to Repent

Heaven and Hell will have it out over my halo someday,
and there's something sobering in that sentiment.

I'm in no rush to repent the things I don't remember,
and I'm juxtaposed at the idea of being judged—
at the prospect of paying my dues to the Devil for what I've done.

The Little Liberations in Acceptance

Omissions.
Simple things we wish we'd said but didn't.
Haven't.

Oversights or under shares, who's to say?
There's little liberations in acceptance,
and I'm putting on my big boy pants.
Pulling myself up by my bootstraps
and coming to terms with curating my own conundrums.

And That Will Be the End of It

When I'm called upon to characterize the curiosity of being a bird,
the marvel of manipulating the breath of a breeze and bursting
thought bubbles of billowing nimbus,
when they plead and beg me recount the wonder of a world beneath
my spirited wing,
I'll smile and fly.

Stars Are Just Convictions Pinned to a Posterboard

Say that you saw
      me
taking a ride through the
      cosmos
and shouted my name,
how the quiet cut you off when you called out.

Say something
      cockamamie
about the vacuous nature of space,
how it's a
      vacuum,
collecting convictions
and pinning them to a pitch-black posterboard.

The World Burns and We Go About Our Business

Fell asleep in a forest fire once to find myself;

               the snap, crackle, and pop
          conversation of caterwauling pines

commiserating their pleas'
skyward rang a series of reverberating piano notes,
      and I profess to tapping an account of their suffering in
overtures of madness.

Love Is a Misfit With a Sidelong Gait

This is the poem stuck in my head:

a bluegrass tune plucked to a time warp tempo,
about a boy and his midnight mongrel,

      "El Perro Negro"

as it circulated amongst the avocado groves;
a misfit mixed breed with a sidelong gait and a penchant
for nipping at the
      San Luis sunshine.

Tell Them How I Tried

Tell them how I tried,
     my loves,
when the tawdry affair of delegating my dust to sputter
and salt of ocean currents comes to pass.

Smart the stars with stanzas that fell short,
so they shine anew on the incomprehensible planes of poetry,
and tell them how I tried,
     loves.

A Poem a Day Keeps the Madness at Bay

It's the work between words,
madness in minutia,
   pulling me from the pen that pains me—little labors that
countdown like contractions, waiting for me to wander back and tie
two things together that aren't atypical of each other.

I'm a storyteller; the rest is bull roar.

FASTER

Freeway speeds
And swinging from the back
Seat, passengers and passing winds, rushing roads and
The rush of riding white lines,
Excitable, yelling at yellow and raising a balled fist to
Red—

jailbird juveniles consummating our peril
and pushing the possibilities; begging to crash.

I've Been Meaning to Mention

How you caught me
from across the room, saw through a hundred thousand idle eyes,
and handed me your heart in a smile.

How you cover yourself
in two tones and carry me
without condition,
    how I'm happy in your reverie—the beauty of birds roaming,
swooping low and lonely.

We Were More Than a Poem (If Only for a Moment)

Kind eyes
and the curve of crimson-stained pale,

can I say a thing aloud,

an allegory about adventuring the backside of underrated albums,
quick quips of hallowed lips,
and Ferris wheel feelings?

Could I properly chronicle the stark contrast between love and
loving you?

Tonight I Don't Bother You With Bad Things

Not tonight,
for reasons all my own,
the shape of constellations and the vulnerability of a bedtime breeze,
will I bother you with bad things—the moribund motorbiker what met
the wrath and rage of pitiless pavement,
how I wept his disposition as we held him;
not tonight.

The Desert Knows Our Dirty Deeds

Dancing

on the edge of a moonbeam blade,
the desert swell's a rising sword,
scoring little nicks on your lover's back.

Mine are the orbs in shadow's glow, playing witness to every parry,
each advance and second intention, breathlessly beholding this
bawdy - bodied tango.

I Take Up the Pen, and Put It Down Again

A letter now to my loved one, but which one?

Maybe one for everyone?

For the ones who are mothers now somewhere else?

For the one that was, the one that is, and the one that will be?

A letter to palms, perhaps?

The pressure in pressed fingers and the penultimate letdown.

The New Ones Will Ask of Loss, and The Old Will Say

How arms coat and comfort,
sweep up and squeeze in the discord of service to the dearly departed.

How a heart is most brave in clutch of tender hands.

How solace found
in something lost only speaks volumes to our strengths.

How the space between
        life and death,
is love.

Scholars Speak of Love Without Authority

What use are words
written by the well-read and wise
of heart-hungry fools who rush in?

The scribbled semantics of sideline spectators sodden with envy,
what use?

I've played the game long and short,
wandered wonderlands
in a pair of eyes,
      and never felt myself the fool.

We Tread in Hum of Morning Hush

We tread in hum of morning hush,
      the hour of birdsong
and sidewalks sighing the cool of irrigation excess.

You say something about nothing,
      an idiom concerning my inattentiveness,
but I'm not listening. Passing halogens prompt us onward; somnolent
rays splay the discord.

Not for Forgiveness, for Release

The blonde one
      with the baby blues,
            or was it emerald green?

Heaven help me,
      I'd give it all for a passing moment,
            one day to do it over, put forward a valiant effort,
and be better with how I go about breaking a heart.

Not to have her as my own, but not to ponder blues.

Drinking and Thinking

Surprise,
   surprise,
there are no surprises anymore.

Bubbles at the bottom of a barrel-bodied wine glass get me thinking:

   how I dared defy the odds this long?

How I ever warded off wandering into the deep end of the gene pool
and drifting away into currents of dependency?

I Give Myself to Waves, to God

Sundown on the shoreline,
a sainted communion

where seascape and skylights
sigh their salutations to the other in tempered sacrament,

let this be the last place I skim the rough of dusted bristle in burdened
reverence and surrender myself a shock wave into omniscience.

Our Final Performance Was a Love Scene

Sometime,
in the eclipse of a high shine,
      when the ambiance of an aboriginal afternoon had come to crest,

      we stole away to walk about, to speak of beauty beyond fear,
but I did not dare think it true lest my hand estrange from yours,
      and I awoke to thundering applause.

Somewhere, She's Under the Blankets

It's the glass hour again,
and you're gone,
fighting feelings of fragility,
hiding you for you, for you from me.

It's the pre-dawn with the lamp on,
ask that I idle, idol you, and hold your heavy.

Hearts like ours beat hard but steady, almost too much,
and never enough.

This Is the Prayer

For desert flowers,
      petals fair,
the prickled barb of cactus arms to keep at bay barren wilds.

     For jaded hearts with fractured parts,
 the salving balm of mending palms to piece anew their whole again.

For mourning suns, lonely ones,
the echo of windswept canyons at dawn.

Some Came Before Us, and Some Before Them

Ash
and bone,

we built our empire on the embers of an earlier fire,
scrawled a story of love and living under the same moon with the
edged ends of charred cortical, traded pains and paid for pleasure in
the tragedy of whispered wanting, and wondered at unspoken endings.

River Palms and Ocean Arms

Steady the run
of refined lines in your river palms
and place them to my ocean arms.

Collective sighs
at your creek bed eyes branch a tributary,
stream and stem as open ends and come back again.

Love is the sensation before the fall—the exhilaration while in it.

I'm Over Thinking

And when I think I think too much,
    I linger on awhile longer,

    scents of sandalwood and
the glimmer of your rose oil skin
    sparkle in the dim of fireflies a-flight.

And when I miss the shape of lips,
    the curve of brows over almond browns,
I muse in overtones of afterglows.

One for Every Ever After

Wishing's best
for wishing your wishes away,
I've everything I ever asked for,
and every ever after;
loved like a domino, set myself up for the inevitable knockdown a
thousand times over and stayed the course, sturdy and steadfast as
the valley streams of sunder.

In Hindsight

The seemingly separate issues of freeway refuse,
the fact that
I'm not aging well over time,
     and the detaching sensation in domesticity.

The allure
     of a veering steering wheel and alloy spark against the
guardrails—objects in the rearview that are closer
than they appear.

Icebergs and Shadows Have an Understanding

Run a weathered thumb
.grain the lipped-rim of your midnight wine glass
.nd consider the implications of icebergs
     and their innate understanding of shadowed things
)elow the surface.

Steady your grogg-eyed gaze,
     mid-swirl coalescing whirl,
          that you don't miss the irony.

Pull

Pull us
playful,
and place us,
canyon etched,
creviced in places,
complacent, sea,
and shore,
the ocean floor,
whitecap drift on currents swift,
breaking bows,
making them,
stern,
steady,
helmed and ready,
rise and fall,
beckon call
to love
and lust,
ash,
and dust,
pull.

How Lovely You Were That Way

Talk me through your two a.m.,
moonlight at midnights are midday reminders of yesterday's makeup,
mile-high wine glasses,
    and missing you.

Sing me a sky full of stars
while smiling;
    I'll share a scene
from a dream,
    dressed white with compliant wildflowers in your hair.

A Query for the Modern Poet

Have not the first men
already penned all that can be said?

What left
but the lull of moon tides
or the probing drift of curious tips the length of a lover's constitution?

Were I born a statistician,
would I be delivered of my cynicism?

And of what would I write then?

Untitled (Much the Same As We Were)

Fetter my eager tongue
that I won't speak the words,
     let slip from
loose lips
       those sainted syllables
and take you by surprise,
unravel the tethered ends and float off into your ephemera.

Dash me as doppelgänger drops of your darkest secrets—
like sand granule sentiments.

Echoing Van Gogh's Sentiments

There were no words without intent,
      no syllable,
      sentence,
      nor scheme rhymed ill of reason.

Whether to weather the melancholy of sea splash effervescence,
      canonize a lover's eyes,
      or flesh out the glory of God's grandeur,
I've bled my eyes at eternity's gate and wrote.

Didn't Land Lead Role of Me Until I Was Already Old

For better

or worse,

that's me in the mirror,

that's me in the rearview

looking back

on a life hard-lived,

on a face earned the hard way,

full of flaws,

reflections,

of a character type,

typecast too many times before landing the role of a lifetime,

his war cry quieted by age.

And so We Remain

Chancing you is questioning the cosmos,
challenging coincidence,
and coming to terms with not knowing
      that I don't know
      that I don't know.

Ignorance is debt
collected with sand dollar currency,
      and so we remain,
      star-crossed and penniless,
without kiss to cash the check.

A Love Poem to Distract From Love Poems

For the sake of not speaking inelegant dialects of another desperate
     love
         poem,
     today

I steel my pen aside and note the char
of sagebrush burn against

  skyline blues, the purposed swoop of the wary sterling,
and acknowledge

    these as the end days of wistful boyish romance.

Now We're Talking

Talking about the technology of tectonics,
plated hearts, and the pursuit of pushing each other's boundaries.

Diverging:
>   detachment and distancing.

Transforming:
>   edging and eddying, elapsing.

Converging:
>   conceding love and coming together,

                        and in the end, an earthquake.

The Moment, the Instant

Looking over every line
and lingering,
learning the touch of blush that pinks your cheeks,
contemplating every curve
that courses the contours uniquely you,
　　　simmering
the smolder of your soft-spoken,
and remembering
　　　the moment
I unraveled—the instant I became enraptured.

A Thing to Know of Wilted Flowers

What a wilted flower wants to say,
        she doesn't.

Settled petals need time
        to perk and stir,
but the Wasatch sun remains
        unchanged,
smiles scattered rays of lambent love
        to drive away the crestfallen clouds,
to shelter her from worry and white noise of windstorms at dark.

All Things Finite Are Condemned to Figment

That sunset you saw,
one summer's eve when you were odd years old,
will never quite recall to conscious as once it did
when you were young.

All things finite
are soon condemned
      to figment,
Illusory,
and elusive
      to the imagination—blackened atrophy to the brackish gloom.

Dirty Dishes Are a Midlife Crisis

Staring down a sink drain backup,
it bubbled up
        and blanketed a soap scum foreshadowing over me
that I couldn't scrub clean.

A knowing,
        clear as mud,
        comprehensive as the crust
and crud coagulate
        that this is what it all amounts to:

                bubbles and scrubbing, crust, and crud.

I'm Breaking Up the Band

In finding my dreams summed
to little more than sandcastle
erosion at the persistence of this
insatiable appetite for chaos that
ceaselessly abides within,
I'll thumb my nose from the dock as
Thoreau did to this construct existence
and find myself civilized in the wild.

Beneath a Timely Pine, They Come to Me

I write for

    lonesome things, the pinecone, undergrown, that let loose too soon.

I write for

    lovers new and old, the hearts I've held, and the ones I hold.

I write for

    newborn mothers, smiles unspoiled;

for

    the freedom of a slow song interlude between tender touch I write.

What Use Are Bones If the Skin Won't Hold?

Overcast oceans aren't so lonely after all.

I'd thought that once,
      hoped it, perhaps,
stood at the edge of salt-nipped sands and shouted
at God to strike me down;

this skin is simply a decoy,
      my soul's as old as time,
and I'm tired, ready to unravel down to weary bones.

When They're Grown

And when the children are full-grown
and fan out on their own,
we'll finally afford flannel,
and boho brimmed things,
skit about in suspendered attire
and sway to the everlasting whistle of a slow train.

I'll hang up the shaving kit,
and you'll wear your hair down
when they're grown.

On Such a Day As This I'll Ask

I set my palms
    in trine,
and place them
to the pouring rain,
would you do the same,

    furrow your forehead to mine
in quiet orison
      and fall back in,
        to love and lust
and the story of us,
          read and write old sins anew,
as lovers do, if I place my palms to rain in trine?

Circus Affair

Carnivals they come and go,
punch a ticket, take the ride,
will yourself to go around again and be merry about it.
Blush your face clown-nose red
and give a honk,
paint your frowns right upside down,
and smile your thanks for all the laughs.

    Carnivals,
they come and go.

Poets Don't Hold Their Peace But Rest in It

I don't say anything;
        we don't,
        people.

Someone said that once,
and now I'm thinking
of the Sextons,
Sylvias,
and so on.

Of Virginia Woolf and pocket stones,
Hemingway on that fateful day,
        wondering
if we live only in the line of a poem
        like
it's forbidden to actually feel something?

Marriage Can Be Lonely at Times

Consummate a c-shape
when you curl your back to mine,
bodies like a butterfly when we sleep;
these are long goodnights with bad dreams for keeping the company.

Funny how an inaffectionate farewell can last forever,
like a lukewarm handshake from a stranger—unforgettable.

Those That Know Will Hang Their Heads

A poem,
for everything they'd like to know
      about the machine,
the pressure of it
      on your patience,

    and how getting by
is just getting up in the morning.

    Sometimes I speak it as a song lyric,
lines of the way life gets to moms and dads,
      the ones before and those to come.

The End Is a Proverb, Hanging From a Cliff

I'm waiting on a weather vein,
stratums of stratus to rupture loose a pocket of desert rain
that will cast down cents of silver dollar wisdom.

I'm waiting,
a horse to water,
to sup sage the brush of wise winds a-slight my puerile cheeks,
but something about leading takes meaning.

Surely This Is Wishful Thinking

Surely the sun has an amusing anecdote about the length of a day,
something stimulating to say of terra firma reform,
or the antagonistic attraction between the moon
and the unyielding tides of lap and loam.
Surely the sun could speak to all things but remains secretive.

Su for Short

Conversations about countenance
      and keeping our heads above the whitecaps,
bad-mouthing your bravery,
and how blessed mothers
      are doomed to compensate the tortured hearts of fathers.

Someday,
      with your say so,
I'll call you Su for short;
      we'll breathe and raze this city.

Weatherman

Conduit of conflict,
conductor of contention,
      I am the wind,
      the rain,
      the summer swell,
      the frosted pane in winter's gale,
      I am the fog,
      the hail,
      and hurricanes,
      the atmosphere when you're afraid,
      the tingle before the typhoon;
      all things elemental—I am the weatherman.

Blush

I want to kiss you like we're kids again,
hold you like we're older,
when it's slower,

when it's matchstick romance,
slow burn,
slow to turn,
candle flame,
before the bang,

after the aftermath and holding tight,
dynamite,
combusting in lusting,

I want to hold you there.

Mind the Creases As You Do

Fold and tuck us
      paper hearts, little scraps of color fused and complimentary,
an origami opus of art,
         work, a labor of love, and place us in your preferred pocket.

Pull us out a handkerchief
         when loneliness weeps the coastline melancholy,
and dab away your salted wet.

A Portrait of Painting on My Public Face

Accouterments of counterfeit contentment,
simulated smiles,
      and pantomiming simple pleasures,
           I wear the history of my hardened heart
       the same way as these whiskey - weary eyes in absentia;
               low and longing,
lush with achromatic color palettes—a smelting of Poe and Van Gogh.

Mayshine Melts the Snow, Exposes Mountain Bone

Were not these the salted crests,
stolen away to runoff
by the comfort of Mayshine merriment,
the splintered-gnarl
of desperate palms rooted stone
and reaching skyward, that called upon your longing sigh,
an oceanside exhalation to lull the lapping tides a-sway your feet?

We, the Bubble Born

Bubble shadows circle the shallow
but never concede the drain;
  would that I were a shadow,
  silhouetted,
sans opacity,
spiraling the safe space of the surface.

Alas,
  I am the latter,
  bubble born,
coalescent, complicated, cursory, bred to burst.

Would that I were a shadow.

Friday Nights Are for Leaning the Seats Back

I'm saving that last line for the nighttime,
        the right time,
for courting thoughts in parking lots,
abstaining refraining with hands on hands,
        and having offhand conversations
that go beyond behaved intentions.

        I'm saving that last line for backseats and bated breathing.

To Whom It May Concern

Got away to dust despair
and dune desolation
where silt and the smooth of sandstone share a currency,

    squared up with the cliff face,
        shoulders straight, and fired off a note of my contempt for this
world into the gaping eye of providence on the wings of a wrist rocket.

For the Record

It was pine shade therapy
and spilling secrets of the summer rain where you live,
the language of humming locomotives,
and scoring symphonies of greyscale in charcoal sketches.

It was the picture perfection of a patio queen and her princess
that put a
smile on my face.

On the Off Chance You Read This

Settling into the open arms of syncope,
the grievous air of cozy-clean,

sandalwood and gardenia,
or the phantom sounds of your footfalls on the front stairs.

Explanations are irrelevant without acknowledgment,
the pretense of permission to say how a thing is and know.

Pat Benatar Put It Perfectly

Battle cries and bloodshed,
love is a life sentence best served embittered,
        sweet,
with a splash of salt to keep war wounds convoluted.

        Taller men walk with chipped-shoulder and talk of time
           and healing,
    some semblance of comfort to bed down with in the dark of night.

Myoclonus

Falling in a dream
and coming to
feels like mariachi midnights,
risked inhibitions at 120 with your
eyes closed and a foot to the floor,

feels like finding it,
      for the first time,
      contact from across the dance hall,
trying not to stare, taking a deep breath, and waking.

Being Happy Is so Last Season

"We'll be better in the morning,"
and other lies we hang up to air out with the afternoon laundry.

Being happy's its own miserable business,
but being satisfied seems entirely unreasonable;
something that went out of style the previous season,
now we assess the new one.

We Go the Way of Creeks and Streams

A river doesn't have the right to say
what fate befalls the earth sprung rain;
      all things eventually venture into eternity,
      even creeks and streams must make their way to astral oceans.

What more
than a passing nod to precipitation will come of us as we course,
      I wonder?

Dusk Settles Over Songs From Our Youth

Cooling on the cusp of the crepuscular,
tinctures of twilight fingertipping you
tones of violet blush against the gentle hush of pre-night.

We're on the edge of something ourselves,
seventeen in a song that sounds hauntingly familiar,
but we're older, and the glow fades.

Alternate Ending

Never you mind now,
           that letter,
the unmarked one,
           opened or not,
it wouldn't matter whether.

Never you mind if I leaned into the

curve of each line with careful consideration
or quietly chalked everything up to coincidence

and coexisting on a contemporaneous timeline.

I Pray My Darlings Kill Me First

What ought a father say of strength
to sons who've the courage yet to dream?

The anecdote of death as a dandelion
and the deeply humorous despair in realizing one
is not without the other?

Such the same as confidence is to childishness,
angst and anger are to age.

Here's Hoping Heaven Is Reliving This Moment

Tramping through two feet of Tahoe,
snowpack store,
and Sugar pine shed,
      an air of ancestry whistled through the Emerald Bay,
      muted musings of lapless shores and the somber tone of
      Vikingsholm, tucked repose and all alone—bone
soak and awe beating away the bitter.

I Write This Poem Potpourri

I write this poem potpourri, withered words,
a touch of wilt and color wash, fruit barren but fragrant,
fitting for filling decorative dishes passed down
from one dead hand to another,
for planting new death as the old ones—something scented for consult,
for consolement.

Qualifying As a Qualifier

Tired's an adjective with
        two sonants
        too many,
being it's a verb,
        a disyllabic state of mind,
        and lately,
I'm a squinting modifier,
dangling over a pocket of exhaustion.

Life's turned out to be a noun,
        hanging around,
keeping some secret under lock and key,
        away from me.

Food for Thought

Cadmium cool
in the long of evening's shadow,
dusk gathers a ball gown brilliance
and casts itself cathedral–curtains of incorporeal crosswise
the valley floor vigilance.

Somewhere on the other side,
    an Emerald Isle island,
she's savoring in synesthesia,
    smiling.

Just Desserts

If it's anything at all,
I've known it chafe
and bitter pill—
cut my teeth on context early to quell the shame of defeat.

Someones' stole this life out from under me
before I broke first bones,
but six feet between boots and burial plots
better even the Devil in the end.

Takes Time, a Life's Worth

The tender age of telling
ourselves we're capable of
becoming anything is everything,

    but building up the confidence to endure
    a relentless state of restlessness takes time,
    a life's worth;

It starts a stream,
his rivulet that ripples a swell
      and soon balloons a deluge.

Musings From the Driveway

Simple sentence sentiments in your driveway,
      from the long day,
head down with hands to dash—little musings
      of missing me still say the most.

How the heart can't help the who for whom
it skips record scratch rhythms that make the
melody slip and stutter, makes me wonder.

As Icarus Did, I Too, Flew Far Higher Than One Should

Although I did not aim,
                     as Icarus did,
awash his hearted-resolve and drunken ambition
                     to curry favor
with eidolons of the upper atmosphere, I, too, loosed aloft words of love
on waxed-winged parchment
heedless the hazards of hubris—the lap of sea lather my penance now.

Simple Things Are Better Saved for Eulogies

Suppose
we save these last few lines
for a better time,
long after it's far too late to lend a hand;
       mother,
       sister,
       daughter,
       friend.

Suppose we normalize suppressed affection for those oppressed with graveside speeches—the simple things said better sooner than later.

Freeway Speed in Slow Motion

And if I close my eyes,
as the blackbird does,
     his face to the afternoon
sun in aimless aviation,
     let loose my hands from the wheel
and petition the pavement for a modicum of compassion,
     will I know the sensation of the wind beneath my wings,
     briefly,
     liberated my feet?

Mary

Sharing the Mother's sainted name
never made her one,
but I could've kept a closer eye
when things got carried away—
boys know nothing of the daughters of fathers.

She has sons of her own now,
      her garden grown,
            quite contrary to the life
                  I thought she'd carve out for herself.

Pondside Contemplations

Pondside contemplations are my preference now,
shallow creeks lack depth, and the rippling prow of a furrowed river
brow offers no opportunity for reflection;

I need the smooth of a glass-steady surface,
steadfast to get a good look at myself pondering,
as I do—pondside.

Am I Older Than the Earth?

Bramble hands
that crack a tangle of flexion creases,
branch away, and bridge the briar between every
evolution etched out over the eons,

am I older now than the earth?
Something unsaid in my soul suggests an air of omniscience, a
knowing line not yet put down in a poem.

Keeping Company

Keeping company
with the
seconds in
the silence
of one
sad song's
ending bemoaning
the beginning
of the
next, we
hesitate here
condemning chorus
and verse,
which one's
worse, surmising
which stanza
she'll show
up in
next; each
line a
lunacy fringe,
we keep
the company.

A Murder of Crows Converge at the Church on 800

Spirits settle shades of sinister
where snow and slope converge,
and the irony of Sunday steeples
shrinking in the loom of circling
crows isn't lost on me.

"Stepping into the flesh of something long-forgotten"
was a line I'd meant to impart
but didn't trust my intuition.

The Age of Silent Suffering

Vapor whorl
that hasn't quite settled,
and already we're unpacking a life's
worth of luggage—a saga of suitcases and two-suiters brimming with
baggage and blistered feels.

November's kinder today
than either can recall,
     yet still,
observe this as the age of silent suffering.

I Wear This Crown of Conceit

God, damn me these passive virtues
but permit me quiet reasoning;
every lash of tongue,
      each instance of insolence
      or word unkind
a point of pride I wore a plume—feathered-pretensions
pressed one
      against the other
to a crown of conceit heavier now than my head can hold.

It Comes Around, and We Do Them Over Again

Monday night Magpies a-light the backyard bird feeder
is Tuesday's bane,
but we laugh it off and load up again.

Wednesday comes
         and goes
with the bore of burnt toast over coffee black,
while Thursday has that Friday feeling
of Saturday evening sacrilege repaid on Sunday.

Something Saccharine Storied Over Stressed Syllables

She shines the shoreline,
      seaside with the sunrise,
      sashays the low swell,
      smiles the high tides,

says something aloud through sealed lips,
the sweet of salt on adequate tongues,
the soft of hands on restless hips,
shimmers the sand wave-swept,
as we step, the shoreline.

ASCII 32

Not so much a rock and a hard place,
but the soft space,
between blue lines on a white page,

those millimeter margins where
new loves are waxed poetic in idyll worship,

and the old ones are memorialized for time
and eternity, a tribute to all that was and never will be.

The Shadow of Age Now Shows in My Smile Lines

A splash of cool
        to ebb out the rough of yesterday's remnants,
                shadows of age and fermentation
showboating a sweeping success in the fine lines
where once a smile occupied—

                "crow's feet," I've heard it called;

    best to linger anything other than the listlessness of sunken lids.

I'm All of This and More

In finalizing my definitive form,
I have become, a bit more than just a father's son,

my mother's mistake,
the words I write, or hearts they break.

I am the sum of setting suns,
the lore of devils in the dusk fall darkness,

and the recompense that
comes at dawn's expense.

We Had, at Least, the Sky

And if at once
the sky's all we've left to muse,
talks of teal
and the temperament of turquoise
brooding beryl,
      contemplating cerulean
      and agonizing azure,

if something so treacherous,
acknowledging we're aged as indigo
ensues while we amble,
we had,
      at least,
the sky.

Empty Eyes on Open Caskets

Sweater weather
and the aroma of everything I thought I'd be by now
      fall
and
      settle with the indifference of
fathers who've nothing of note to tell of their fathers,
grim men are oft not glib, as they say—empty eyes on open caskets
haunt me in the still hours,

    and I weep.

What I Could Have Done, I Should Have

The parting is oft not so sweet as the sorrow,
I find, and there's no soft way to sugarcoat
how hard bad goodbyes can be.

Kinder souls more considerate than myself
would've put up a front, painted their faces brave,
and pulled themselves together for a friend's farewell.

Elements of My Ancestry Are Long Dusted and Dead

In time
I may come to forgive
the significance of antiquated notions
collecting layers of sift
and secrecy in the shelved-silence of storage closets;
      canned goods and collectibles
cubbyholed away by design
and without accident—the anticipation of becoming an apparition.

Awfully Lonely (Marriage Can Be)

A.M. pavement gleans

"good morning"

in the smile of a Utah County sunrise;
imagine me,
on the run,
from what I cannot say,
but I'm not too shy
to talk about the way you cradled the dog with your back to
my
belly that night,
the battle over, and the war still far from it.

Psalm 116:3

The bridge a-gap this astral plane
          of peace
                    and Hell
begins with a door,
and turning my time
 and attention over to a tire fire traumatist
  was the distempered hysteria of fifth symphony timpani—

          budding madness Beethoven himself could not have
                    orchestrated so theatrically.

Daddy's Hands

Powder fresh prints
are an epiphany—a page marked intimately
by blanket drift and dawdled boots.

I'd thought this scene significant once,
the inscape of affection even,
sun-spangle on snowpack with sprinklings of juniper shed,
and my budding hand awaiting his in earnest.

Hallway Sex Isn't All It's Cracked Up to Be

Speaking our frustrations
through sidelong glances and silence,

soft-spoken salutations in passing
will suffice after a late evening of

screaming and sleeplessness—anything to expedite the exasperation of
experiencing emotions ere the early morning Earl Grey and eggs.

Beyond the Frosted Veil

Beyond the frosted veil,
I mind the charge of sleet - crusted poplars,
sentinels looming a disquieting silhouette,
their branched hands an icy armament
against the fret of phantoms idle.

Surely there are ghosts of grand delusion
that reside in this limbus, beyond the veil.

People, Are.

People,
      are.

Feigned interest in anything worthwhile
      keeps me from finishing that thought;

adult - onset disappointment,
      gore,
      God,
      guilt,
      aspirations abridged in early adolescence,
ward off any wishing there was more to say,
but it suffices to put it simply:

people,
      are.

A Year of Wine and Loose Leaves

This will be the year of finding my faults in the flavors
of fine wine and post-sex small talk cigarettes.

This will be the night I peer up at a thumbnail moon and test my
temperament, let my tequila tongue talk me into trouble,
and satisfy my hunger for self-destruction.

    Loose leaves are lonely; I realize that now.
        Takes a wind scattered thing to know another,
            to recognize the plight of the boundless,
                unbridled from the bosom of the mother branch,
                  surrendered to the insincerity of an
                    overcast sun,
swirling its avarice as stormcloud swill.

How Clever, the Cosmos, With It's Secrets Vast

Storied runes
of the long-suffering
scrawled crossways along the stars,
        we,
students of self-examination,
curious of the cosmos
        and all of its coveted complexities,
gazing aloft to the twinkling of celestial beacons,
longing a sense of propriety,
        to signify our purpose.

Before You Go

And you will, sure as the mighty river breaks for the ocean by way o
least resistance, you too will take up the blacktop and pave a path t
places unknown, keeping the sacrality of shouting matches betweer
yourself and highway winds a secret as you do.

I'll put down in various poems, before such a time comes, what I'd hopec
wanted, and wished to say, leaving them mile markers along the road o
life, living mine in the rearview knowing that looking forward is fo
those who've not yet found their reflection.

Acknowledgments

To my family, friends, and amazing followers, I must express eternal gratitude. Your tireless support lifts my spirits daily and continues to give me strength and inspiration in my endeavors and writing. I truly could not chase my dreams without your love. If my words have reached you in any way, please, kindly leave a review for this book. Your time and thoughts are important to me.

Printed in Great Britain
by Amazon

29865173R00099